AWESOME SUPER SIMPLE
HABITAT PROJECTS

# SUPER SIMPLE

# FARM

# PROJECTS

## FUN & EASY ANIMAL ENVIRONMENT ACTIVITIES

### CAROLYN BERNHARDT

CONSULTING EDITOR, DIANE CRAIG, M.A./READING SPECIALIST

**Super Sandcastle**

An Imprint of Abdo Publishing
abdopublishing.com

# abdopublishing.com

Published by Abdo Publishing, a division of ABDO, PO Box 398166, Minneapolis, Minnesota 55439. Copyright © 2017 by Abdo Consulting Group, Inc. International copyrights reserved in all countries. No part of this book may be reproduced in any form without written permission from the publisher. Super SandCastle™ is a trademark and logo of Abdo Publishing.

Printed in the United States of America, North Mankato, Minnesota
102016
012017

Editor: Liz Salzmann
Content Developer: Nancy Tuminelly
Cover and Interior Design and Production: Mighty Media, Inc.
Photo Credits: Mighty Media, Inc.; Shutterstock

The following manufacturers/names appearing in this book are trademarks: Altoids®, Craft Smart®, Crayola®, Elmer's® Glue-All®, Sharpie®

**Publisher's Cataloging-in-Publication Data**

Names: Bernhardt, Carolyn, author.
Title: Super simple farm projects: fun & easy animal environment activities / by Carolyn Bernhardt.
Other titles: Fun & easy animal environment activities | Fun and easy animal environment activities
Description: Minneapolis, MN : Abdo Publishing, 2017. | Series: Awesome super simple habitat projects
Identifiers: LCCN 2016944667 | ISBN 9781680784404 (lib. bdg.) | ISBN 9781680797930 (ebook)
Subjects: LCSH: Habitats--Juvenile literature. | Habitat (Ecology)-- Juvenile literature. | Farm ecology--Juvenile literature.
Classification: DDC 577--dc23
LC record available at http://lccn.loc.gov/2016944667

Super SandCastle™ books are created by a team of professional educators, reading specialists, and content developers around five essential components—phonemic awareness, phonics, vocabulary, text comprehension, and fluency—to assist young readers as they develop reading skills and strategies and increase their general knowledge. All books are written, reviewed, and leveled for guided reading, early reading intervention, and Accelerated Reader™ programs for use in shared, guided, and independent reading and writing activities to support a balanced approach to literacy instruction.

# To Adult Helpers

The projects in this book are fun and simple. There are just a few things to remember to keep kids safe. Some projects require the use of sharp objects. Also, kids may be using messy materials such as glue or paint. Make sure they protect their clothes and work surfaces. Review the projects before starting, and be ready to assist when necessary.

....................................

## KEY SYMBOL

Watch for this warning symbol in this book. Here is what it means.

### SHARP!
You will be working with a sharp object. Get help!

# CONTENTS

# FED BY FARMS!

**H**ave you ever had a cold glass of milk? Or a crispy piece of chicken? You were eating food from a farm! Farms are very important. They feed us all.

It is important that farmers work to keep the animals they raise healthy. This is because caring for animals responsibly is the **humane** thing to do. It is also important because healthy animals produce the best food.

**MILK FROM A DAIRY FARM**

**CHICKEN FROM A POULTRY FARM**

## FARM ANIMALS

Many amazing animals live on farms. Cows, pigs, chickens, sheep, and more can be found on farms.

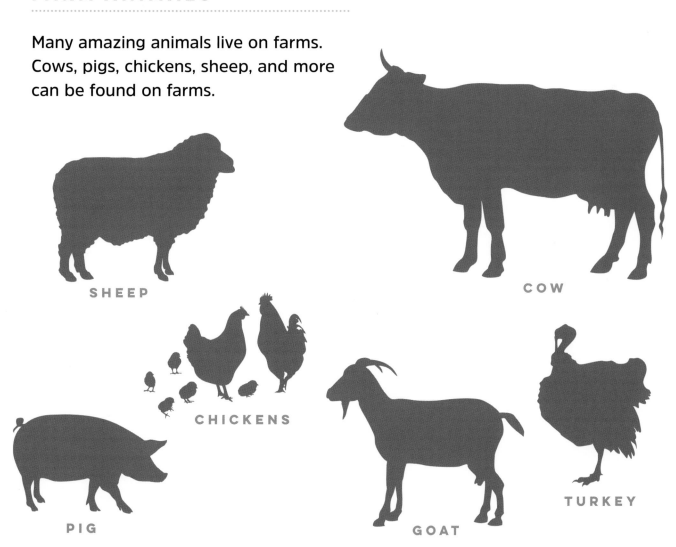

SHEEP

COW

CHICKENS

PIG

GOAT

TURKEY

# HARD WORK
## PAYS OFF

Every farm is different. This is because farms **specialize** in the kinds of food they produce. Dairy farmers raise cows for their milk. Pig farmers raise pigs for their meat. Poultry farmers raise chickens and other birds for eggs or meat.

Food doesn't just appear in your kitchen. Everything you eat is the result of lots of hard work on farms! Farmers wake up very early in the morning to get started. Cows need to be milked. Chicken eggs need to be collected. Tools need to be cleaned and fixed.

COWS BEING MILKED

## ALL IN THE FAMILY

There are more than 2 million farms in the United States! Most of these farms are family owned and operated. Farm and ranch families make up about 2 percent of the US population.

# HABITAT
## FOOD CHAIN

**E**very natural **habitat** has a food chain. The food chain shows what each animal eats. Farms are not natural habitats. They are created by humans. So most animals on farms are not part of a food chain. But they still have to eat!

## FARM ANIMAL DIETS

Most farm animals live in separate areas and are fed by the farmers. Each animal eats something different. Most farm animals are either herbivores or omnivores. Herbivores are animals that only eat plants. Omnivores are animals that eat plants and meat.

### PIGS

Pigs are omnivores. They eat food waste. They eat fruits, vegetables, and meat scraps.

## ANIMAL ADVOCATE

Dr. Temple Grandin is a professor of animal science. She works at Colorado State University in Fort Collins, Colorado. She has created many new ways for beef farmers to handle their cattle. Farmers all over the world use her methods. Grandin has improved animal farming around the world!

### CHICKENS

Chickens are omnivores. Their feed is made of plants and fish meal. Chickens also eat seeds, insects, mice, and even lizards!

### SHEEP

Sheep are herbivores. Sheep **graze** throughout the day. They eat grass, weeds, clover, and other ground plants.

### COWS

Cows are herbivores. A dairy cow eats up to 100 pounds (45 kg) of food each day! The food is usually made up of hay and grains.

# MATERIALS

Here are some of the materials that you will need for the projects in this book.

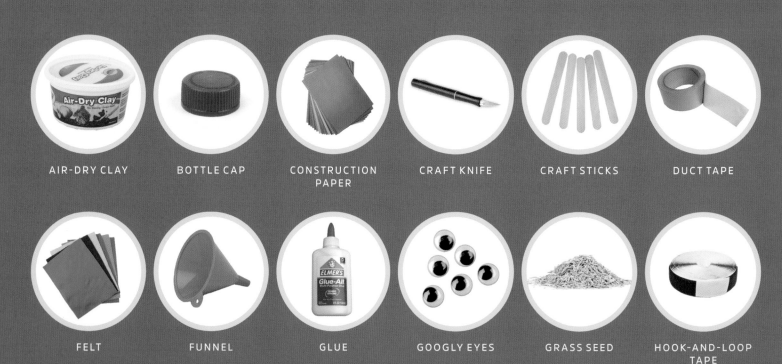

AIR-DRY CLAY

BOTTLE CAP

CONSTRUCTION PAPER

CRAFT KNIFE

CRAFT STICKS

DUCT TAPE

FELT

FUNNEL

GLUE

GOOGLY EYES

GRASS SEED

HOOK-AND-LOOP TAPE

MARKER

METAL BOX
WITH LID

NYLON STOCKINGS

PAINT

PAINT PENS

PAINTBRUSH

PLASTIC CONTAINER
WITH LID

RUBBER BANDS

RULER

SAND

SCISSORS

SMALL BOWLS

SMALL MILK CARTON
WITH SPOUT

SPOON

SPRAY BOTTLE

SPRING
CLOTHESPINS

SQUARE GIFT BOX
WITH A FOLDING LID

UNPOPPED
POPCORN

# BARN OWL
# DISPLAY

**MATERIALS:** small milk carton with spout, paint, paintbrush, white paint pen, box lid, unpopped popcorn, plastic barn owl, farm figurines

**M**ost animals that live on farms are **domesticated**. But some wild animals live on farms too. One such animal is the barn owl. These owls make nests in quiet places, such as old barns. Owls help farmers by eating mice and other farm pests.

## MAKE A MINI FARM!

1. Paint the carton red. Let it dry.

2. Draw the door and window with a white paint pen. Let it dry.

3. Fill the box lid with unpopped popcorn.

4. Place the owl on the milk carton's spout.

5. Set the barn in the box lid. Place other farm figurines in the barnyard.

# GRASSY STOCKING
# SHEEP

**MATERIALS:** small bowls, measuring cup, sand, grass seed, spoon, nylon stocking, scissors, funnel, felt (black, white & pink), glue, googly eyes, hook-and-loop tape, water, spray bottle

Farmers raise sheep for their wool, meat, and milk. These animals live in groups called flocks. Living in flocks makes sheep feel safe from predators. Sheep eat a lot of grass and other plants. They **graze** for about seven hours a day.

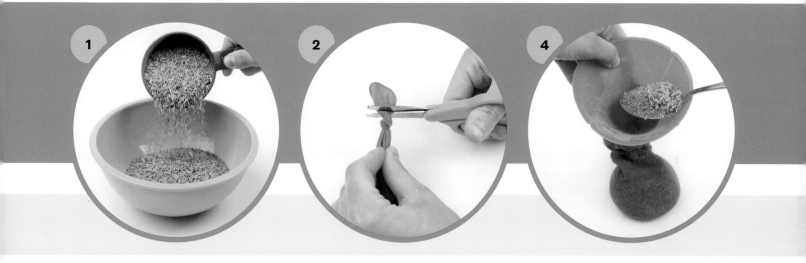

# MAKE A SHEEP OF GRASS!

1  Mix 1 cup of sand with 1 cup of grass seed.

2  Cut the toe off of the stocking. Tie the end in a knot. Pull it tight. Cut off the extra stocking near the knot.

3  Put the funnel into the open end of the stocking.

4  Add the sand and seed mixture.

*Continued on the next page.*

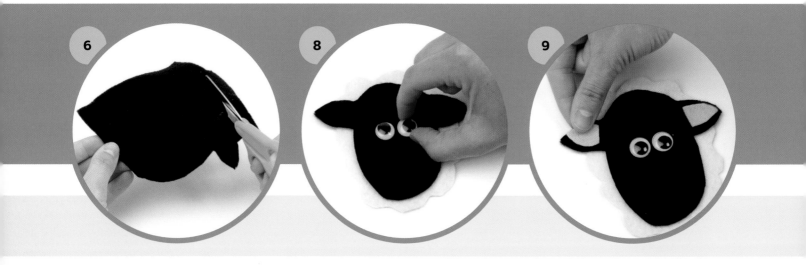

## GRASSY STOCKING SHEEP (CONTINUED)

(5) Tie a knot to close the stocking. Pull it tight. Cut off the extra stocking.

(6) Cut a sheep face out of black felt.

(7) Cut a wavy oval out of white felt. Make it a little bigger than the face. Glue the face to the white shape.

(8) Glue on googly eyes.

(9) Cut small ear and nose shapes out of pink felt. Glue them to the face.

10 Cut a square of hook-and-loop tape. Stick one side to the stocking ball. Stick the other side to the back of the sheep's face.

11 Put the ball in a bowl of water. Make sure it gets thoroughly wet.

12 Pour out the water. Set the bowl near a sunny window. Attach the face.

13 Once a day, take the face off and spray the ball with water. Watch your sheep grow thick, grassy wool!

# SLOPPY CROPS
# COMPOST

**MATERIALS:** plastic container with lid, paint pens, food scraps for composting

Pig farmers feed their pigs special pig food. But some farmers give their pigs **leftover** food scraps too. Pigs aren't picky. Leftover human food is a treat for them.

## RECYCLE FOOD WASTE!

1 Decorate the outside of the plastic container with paint pens.

2 Collect food scraps throughout the week. Put them in your container.

3 If you know a pig farmer, ask if the pigs would like your slop. Otherwise, you could put your scraps in a **compost** bin. They will turn into dirt for gardening!

# COW HUG MACHINE

**MATERIALS:** glue, wide craft sticks, green construction paper, spring clothespins, scissors, narrow craft sticks, duct tape, mini dowels, ruler, felt, plastic cow, rubber band

**M**any farmers use a device called a squeeze chute to help calm scared cattle. It gently squeezes the animals on either side. This comforts them and makes them feel safe.

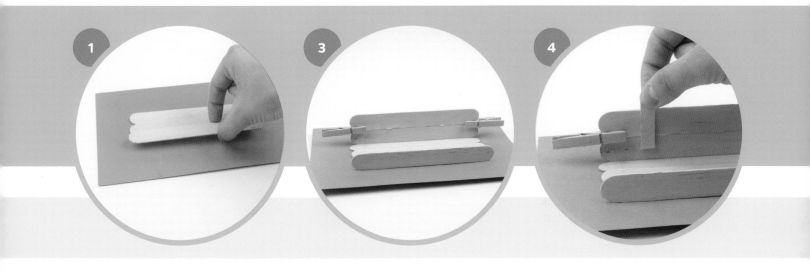

## GIVE A COW A HUG!

① Glue three wide craft sticks side by side to the green paper. This is the base.

② Glue a wide craft stick to each side of the base. Let the glue dry.

③ Glue another wide craft stick on top of one of the sides. Use clothespins to hold it while the glue dries.

④ Cut two pieces of narrow craft stick. Make them as long as the side is tall. Glue them vertically across the side sticks. This will make the side sturdier.

⑤ Repeat steps 3 and 4 on the other side of the base.

⑥ Cut a strip of duct tape the length of a narrow craft stick. Cut the tape in half lengthwise.

*Continued on the next page.*

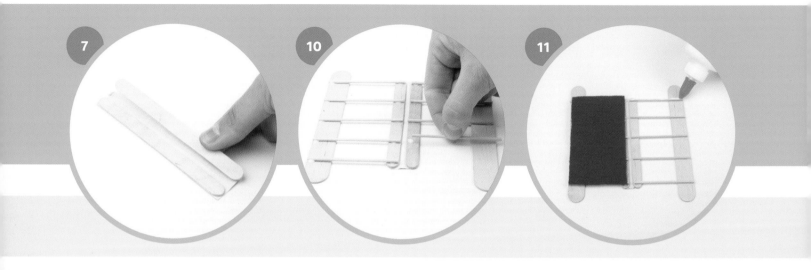

## COW HUG MACHINE (CONTINUED)

⑦ Lay one half of the tape down sticky side up. Set two narrow craft sticks next to each other on the tape. Make sure there is a slight gap between them.

⑧ Place a wide craft stick on each side of the narrow craft sticks.

⑨ Cut ten 2½-inch (6 cm) mini dowels.

⑩ Glue the dowel pieces between the narrow and wide craft sticks. Space them evenly. Let the glue dry. This is the frame.

⑪ Cut two rectangles out of felt. Make them each 2½ by 4½ inches (6 by 11 cm). Glue the felt pieces across each side of the frame. Let the glue dry.

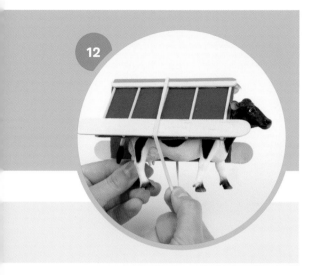

Squeeze chutes are used when an animal needs special care. A cow doesn't understand what the farmer or veterinarian is going to do to it. So, the cow gets scared and resists. Using a squeeze chute calms the cow and holds it still. It is safer for the cow and the people.

**12** Place the hugger over the cow. Use a rubber band to secure the hugger to the cow. This will cause the frame to squeeze the cow gently. Set the cow on the base.

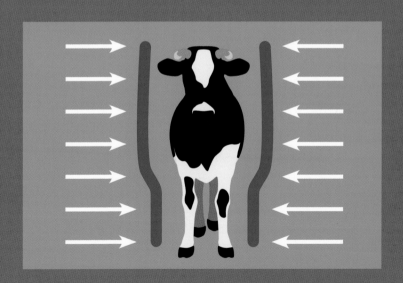

# MINI
# PIGPEN

**MATERIALS:** air-dry clay, metal box
with lid, brown paint, paintbrush,
plastic pig, sand, 2 bottle caps,
water, unpopped popcorn

**D**id you know that pigs don't
sweat? Instead, they roll around
in mud to stay cool. But pigs also
need to be guarded from the hot
sun. The mud covers them to shield
their skin!

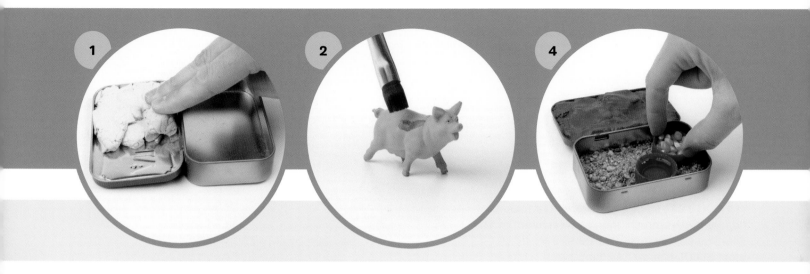

## GIVE A PIG A HOME!

1 Press air-dry clay into the lid of the box. Keep it lumpy to look like mud. Let it dry.

2 Paint the clay brown. Add a few spots of brown paint to the pig. Let the paint dry.

3 Put sand in the bottom of the box.

4 Put water in a bottle cap. Put unpopped popcorn in the other bottle cap. Place them in the box. These are the pig's food and water.

5 Place the pig in its pen!

### DIGGING DEEPER

Mud keeps pigs cool and free of sunburn. But many farmers also use machines to sprinkle pigs with water. The water cools the pigs the same way our sweat cools us!

# COZY CHICKEN COOP

**MATERIALS:** square gift box with a folding lid, paint, paintbrush, marker, ruler, craft knife, wire screen, scissors, duct tape, craft sticks, glue, pencil, electric tea light, plastic chickens

There are more chickens on Earth than any other kind of bird. Most chickens live on farms. Many of these farms have chicken coops for the chickens to live in. Chicken coops keep chickens happy and healthy.

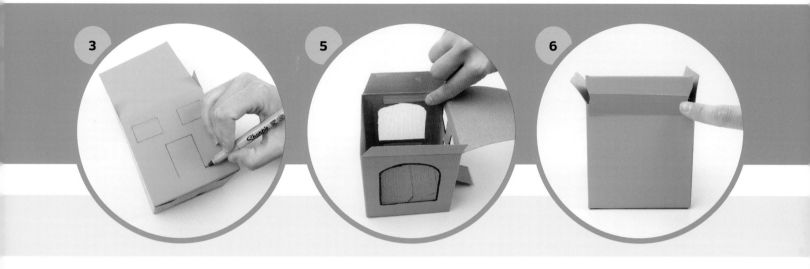

# GIVE CHICKENS A PLACE TO ROOST!

① Paint the box. Let the paint dry.

② Open the box. The side the lid is attached to will be the front of the coop. Draw two windows on the front. Draw a window on each side.

③ Draw a door on the front. The door should be about ½ inch (1 cm) from the bottom.

④ Have an adult help you use the craft knife. Cut out the windows. Cut along the sides and top of the door. Leave the bottom uncut. Fold the door down to form a ramp.

⑤ Tape pieces of screen over each window inside the box.

⑥ Tape the flap on the lid to the top of the box. This makes a slanted roof.

*Continued on the next page.*

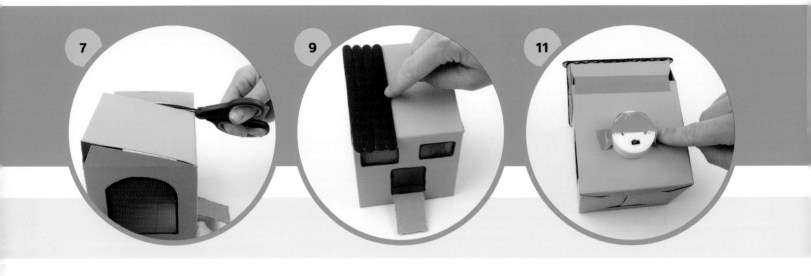

⑦ Trim the side flaps along the top of the roof.

⑧ Set craft sticks side by side on the roof. Decide how many you will need to cover the roof. Remove the sticks and paint them. Let the paint dry.

⑨ Glue the craft sticks to the roof. Let the glue dry.

⑩ Poke a hole in the back of the box with a pencil.

⑪ Push the tea light's bulb through the hole. Tape it in place. Leave the switch uncovered so you can turn the light on and off.

⑫ Place the chickens in and around their coop!

Chickens eat and sleep in their coops. But coops also give chickens space to lay eggs. Most farmers have nesting boxes in their coops. These boxes are where the chickens lay their eggs. Nesting boxes need to be clean, dry, and dark. Otherwise the hens will not feel comfortable laying eggs in them. If a chicken is under stress or not fed correctly, it will not lay eggs. Coops have to be just right for chickens to feel safe and comfortable!

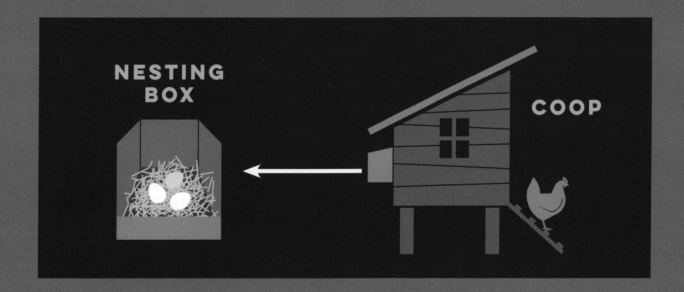

# CONCLUSION

arm animals serve a great purpose. They provide food for everyone in the world! These animals need to be fed and cared for in certain ways in order to do so. This book is the first step in learning more about farming and ranching. There is so much more to find out!

Do you live on or near a farm? Have you ever visited one? Go to the library to **research** farms and farming practices at the library. Or have an adult help you research farms **online**. Learn about different kinds of farms and how farm animals are raised!

# QUIZ

(1) What kind of farm raises cows for their milk?

(2) What is a herd of sheep called?

(3) A squeeze chute is for cattle. TRUE OR FALSE?

## THINK ABOUT IT!

Do you know what farms the food you eat comes from?

Answers: 1. A dairy farm   2. A flock   3. True

# GLOSSARY

**compost** – a mixture of natural materials, such as food scraps and lawn clippings, that can turn into fertilizer over time.

**domesticated** – raised by humans instead of in the wild.

**graze** – to eat growing grasses and plants.

**habitat** – the area or environment where a person or animal usually lives.

**humane** – kind or gentle to people or animals.

**leftover** – something remaining.

**online** – connected to the Internet.

**pasture** – land where animals feed on grass and other plants.

**research** – to find out more about something.

**specialize** – to pursue one branch of study, called a specialty. A person who does this is a specialist.